THE RASCALS
for the Environment
The Stranger

Susan E. Steverman
illustrated by Michael E. O'Hern

NORTH COUNTRY BOOKS
Utica, New York

THE RASCALS
for the Environment
The Stranger

Copyright © 2003
by North Country Books

ISBN 0-925168-85-8

NORTH COUNTRY BOOKS
311 Turner Street
Utica, New York 13501

TABLE OF CONTENTS

RONNIE RABBIT PULLED THE QUILL
FROM MS. PRICKLES' BACK

The Blueberry Lesson

"Ouch!" yelled Ms. Prickles. "Will you hurry up back there?"

"Just one more second, Ms. P.," Ronnie grunted. "Oomph! There, I got it!" He shouted and hopped about (as rabbits tend to do), while holding up the quill that he had just yanked from the back of his porcupine friend.

"I'm not so sure I like what you two are doing, Ronnie," said Ms. Prickles.

As the leader of the Rascals for the Environment crew she wasn't normally one for trickery. Still, Ronnie Rabbit and his pal Billy Bob Bobcat were forever pulling pranks on the other members of the Rascals' gang.

"Come on, Ms. P.," Ronnie said affectionately as he and Billy Bob gathered some leaves from the forest floor. "Bandit deserves this. She's been behaving like a typical raccoon for days now, the way she's been collecting all of the blueberries behind our backs and keeping them for herself."

"Okay, Ronnie," Ms. Prickles said. "But how is one of my quills going to make her share?"

BANDIT MERRILY SINGS UNAWARE OF WHAT LURKS AHEAD

Ronnie turned around to face her. He had just finished placing the collected leaves onto the spot Bandit visited every morning to eat blueberries.

"Don't you see?" Ronnie asked. "When Bandit comes hobbling over and sits on top of these leaves she's going to get the surprise of her life. She'll jump so high that all the berries she's holding will go flying into the air."

"Then all of us will come out of hiding, grab as many as possible and stuff them into our mouths," Billy Bob added.

"Speak for yourselves, you two," Ms. Prickles declared. "I'll have nothing more to do with this."

A few feet away, standing on top of a hollow log, Chippy the chipmunk adjusted his ball cap and called over to Ronnie in a loud whisper. He said he had just caught a glimpse of Bandit plodding through the woods in their direction.

Ronnie quickly placed the quill under some leaves with the pointed end sticking up.

Ms. Prickles rolled her eyes and lumbered off.

Ronnie called out to the rest of the gang, "Okay, everyone, take your places!"

The woodland animals quickly dodged into different hiding spots. Some hid behind trees. Others dove into bushes. Everyone grew quiet. Soon they heard Bandit leisurely making her way through the woods. As she drew closer to her friends they could hear her cheerfully singing:

"Blackberries, raspberries, yum, yum, yum,
But blueberries are the favorite of my tum, tum, tum....
I should be sharing them with all of my buddies,
But I can't help it they go right to my tummy!"

Bandit, her arms full of blueberries, came waddling up to her favorite spot to sit and eat. The other Rascals peered out from their hiding places and watched as their friend slowly turned herself around, and began to lower her rather large backside down onto the quill. The Rascals held their breath.

Then, just before contact, two loud noises suddenly echoed throughout the forest – bang, bang!

ROUGHHOUSE POINTS OUT MOVEMENT
IN THE FOREST WHILE BANDIT LOOKS ON

What's in the Woods?

"**W**hat in the blooming daisies was that?" Ronnie shouted, his whiskers quivering. He was so startled at hearing the loud noise that, without thinking, he had leaped straight up out of the bush where he was hiding.

The rabbit's sudden action spooked Bandit more than the two noises. The raccoon jumped, threw her armload of berries into the air, and rocketed up the nearest tree trunk.

A shower of blueberries began falling like raindrops. Too frightened of what might be in the woods, all the animals could do was look helplessly from their hiding spots over at the plump berries that were now scattered about on the ground.

From high up in the tree, Bandit looked down and realized that it was only Ronnie who had startled her. She began to grow suspicious.

"What were you doing hiding in that bush?" Bandit hollered.

"Shhh!" hushed Ms. Prickles, who had run back to the others after hearing the noise. "Listen."

They quietly froze. Ronnie's long ears perked up like an

antenna. He was the first to hear the sounds of twigs snapping and of dry leaves crunching. The sounds grew closer. Billy Bob moved between Ronnie and Ms. Prickles. "What could it be?" he whispered.

"I don't know," Ms. Prickles told the anxious bobcat. "It's not like anything I've ever heard before."

Patience, the only deer in the group, softly suggested, "Maybe it's those Freebooters who came to the Adirondacks last year."

The Rascals then recalled the rowdy group of men who entered their forest the previous summer, allowed fires to burn uncontrollably, shot at any animal that crossed their path, and left litter throughout the woods.

As the others were busy remembering the Freebooters' poor behavior, Bandit noticed that Patience had managed to edge her way close to the fallen berries and was now nibbling at the fruit. This got her goat!

As the raccoon sat up in the tree blowing smoke over somebody else eating her berries, Roughhouse excitedly called. "I see something! I see something!" The squirrel peered from a perch atop one of the tallest trees. Now there was movement to go along with the noises.

Bandit, anxious to get down from her perch and reclaim her berries, snapped at Roughhouse. "Listen, chatterbox, just tell us what it is!"

Ms. Prickles quieted the raccoon with a stern look and asked the squirrel to continue.

"From what I can see between the trees," Roughhouse said, "it looks as if it's something really big! Bigger than a bear!"

"Really?" Ronnie eagerly asked. "What else?"

Roughhouse began jumping about on his branch, "It's stomping its feet and thrashing its arms!" He exaggerated, only too happy to be the center of attention.

Roughhouse's description of the creature in the woods caused panic and confusion among the animals. They came out of hiding and began running wildly about, bumping into each other. Then, through an opening in the trees, the creature stepped forth...

RONNIE ATTEMPTS TO TRIP THE STRANGER

Getting a Closer Look

After barely glimpsing what had entered the clearing, the Rascals quickly scampered back into hiding. Once hidden, each one slowly peeked out to find a bewildering sight. According to the squirrel's claims, the gathering had envisioned a frightful monster. Instead, what they saw was a thin elderly man sporting a long white beard and carrying some long wooden poles.

The Rascals looked at one another, then turned to glare up at Roughhouse.

The squirrel grinned sheepishly and shrugged his shoulders.

"Who is he?" Ronnie whispered to Ms. Prickles. "And what do you think he's doing with those poles?"

"I don't know," Ms. Prickles said slowly, "but the loud noises that we heard must have come from those poles banging up against the trees."

"He doesn't look like one of those Freebooters," Patience said.

"I wonder what he's doing here?" asked Chippy, as he adjusted his disheveled cap.

"I bet he's come for my blueberries!" sulked the raccoon, who was pouting over her recent loss.

"I can't believe that you're still whining about those berries!" Ronnie huffed.

Ms. Prickles was quiet for a moment. She was quite curious about this new fellow. "How can we get a closer look at this stranger without giving ourselves away?"

The Rascals all thought about it.

Suddenly, Ronnie's whiskers flickered, his ears twitched, and his eyes widened. He whispered into Ms. Prickles' ear. She nodded and he quickly hopped over to a clump of ferns. As the old man began to pass, the rabbit limbered his leg and stuck out his foot.

The animals, amazed at their friend's courage, waited anxiously for the big fall. But instead of tripping over the rabbit's foot, the man came to a stop, glanced down, then stepped casually over the hairy limb and continued up the path.

As the stranger moved away, the gang let out a collective sigh. They decided to follow the newcomer while remaining a safe distance behind. But every once in a while the white-bearded old man would stop and slowly turn around, as if he knew he was being followed.

Following the Stranger

The stranger led the Rascals through the deep forest until they came upon a clearing above a river. The gang was stunned to discover what looked like six tall beaver lodges all clumped together. They watched as the man placed his wooden poles up against one of the woodpiles. He then walked over to another and disappeared inside.

"Those piles look familiar," whispered Ronnie.

"They're called wigwams," Ms. Prickles replied. "The natives used to build them to live in a long time ago."

The animals waited and watched, they saw the old man come out of the wigwam and walk over to a tiny hut located in the middle of all the wigwams. That's when Billy Bob noticed some writing above the hut's doorway.

"Hey, what do you think that sign says?" the bobcat asked.

"I don't know," Ms. Prickles answered. "We need Hoot to help us with this."

Everyone agreed. The owl was the only member of the Rascals gang who could read.

THE RASCALS FOLLOW THE STRANGER
TO A CLEARING

Ms. Prickles asked Robin, another Rascal gang member who had been perched quietly atop Patience's back, if she would fly over and get Hoot.

"No problem, Ms. P.," she replied, "but you know how he is when roused from sleep after a busy night of hunting."

The animals didn't have long to wait before Robin returned with Hoot. Robin gracefully swooped down on Patience's head, but Hoot, still groggy from being so rudely awakened, came in for a crash landing smack dab in the middle of a thorn bush. Letting out a loud squawk, he tumbled from the bramble, and landed in plain view of the stranger's hut.

The animals turned to see whether the old man had seen this mishap. They were relieved to find him heading in the opposite direction toward the river.

HOOT'S CRASH LANDING

While Hoot straightened his feathers, Ms. Prickles filled him in on all that was happening.

"So, you all think this sign will offer a clue as to who our stranger is?" Hoot asked.

"We hope so," Ms. Prickles replied.

The owl proceeded to pull out a pair of oversize black-rimmed spectacles from under his wing. Hoot had discovered the eyeglasses in the woods a few years back. They had been left behind by a child whose family had been camping in the Adirondack mountains. The owl insisted that they improved his near-perfect vision.

As Hoot placed the spectacles atop his nose, his head swiveled toward the hut. He cleared his throat, then majestically read off the words.

"MAYOR OF COLD RIVER."

Exploring the Wigwams

"Mayor of Cold River," the Rascals repeated in unison.

"What does that mean?" Chippy asked.

"Well," Ms. Prickles said. "Cold River, of course, is the river that flows through our valley."

"Then *Mayor* must be the name of our stranger!" Bandit interrupted.

"I think you may be right," said Ms. Prickles, nodding her head thoughtfully.

Ms. Prickles suggested that since Mayor was out of sight the moment was ripe to investigate his camp.

Feeling a burst of bravery, Billy Bob shouted, "I'll do it!" when Ms. Prickles asked for a volunteer. He began to boast, "I have the slyness it takes to get in and out of there unnoticed."

Ms. Prickles cautioned Billy Bob to be careful as he made his way into the clearing. As he crept close to the ground, working his way slowly through some tall grass, he came across a garden plot. He stopped, raised his head, and took in a long sniff of sweet-smelling air. Not only had he just discovered flowers and vegetables growing, but also, lo and behold, blueberries!

Better not tell Bandit about this, he thought to himself. *She'd most likely risk our lives just for a taste.*

Billy Bob left the garden and moved toward the wigwams. He noticed that above three of the entryways there were more signs. He signaled over to Hoot to read them. The owl obliged. One sign read, "The Beauty Parlor." Another read, "Mrs. Rondeau's Kitchenette" and, lastly, there was "Pyramid of Giza."

Billy Bob began exploring the insides of the wigwams. One had kitchenware, another had a tin washbasin and a hollowed-out cedar stump, but the one that was able to double the length of Billy Bob's tail hair was the Pyramid of Giza, which was empty except for a thick noose hanging down from above.

Frightened, he left the wigwam. As a light wind blew, he heard what sounded like rattling. He followed the hollow sound to the side of the hut, where he saw something swaying in the breeze. Inching closer he suddenly realized what it was.

Animal bones!

The bobcat stopped dead in his tracks. His fur stood on end, and his eyes grew wide as he slowly began to back up. Then, turning ever so slightly, he caught sight of some steel traps hanging from nails on the front of the wigwam. Billy Bob's bravery and slyness turned to clumsiness. As he tried to make a run for it he ended up smashing into a rocking chair. A deerskin hide that was on the chair flew off and landed on top of his head.

He was trapped underneath!

BILLY BOB STOPS DEAD IN HIS TRACKS

17

Struggling to pull the cover off, he caught sight of Mayor making his way back from the river. After pushing and pulling, with a final tug he was free. Frantically, he darted into the wigwam and found the darkest corner. His heart still raced but he felt safe for the moment and took a look around the room. It was quite sparse. The only furnishings were a cast iron box stove, a table, and a small bed with a bearskin blanket. That's when Billy Bob spotted some sort of carrying case made out of buckskin.

Does the Mayor make everything out of animal hide, he wondered. Curious, he decided to investigate the carrying case. He gave it a hefty shove and down it went to the floor. A rather ominous looking bow and arrow spilled out at his feet.

At this point he didn't care whether Mayor saw him or not; he just knew he had to get out of there. He bolted through the door, ran wildly across the clearing, crying hysterically.

The Rascals stood in horror as they watched Mayor stop and stare at the bobcat making his mad dash for safety.

Back to the Hangout

As soon as Billy Bob came bounding into the bushes after fleeing from Mayor's camp, he came face to face with a grinning rabbit.

"Now, tell us again about how sly the cat family is?"

Still very shaken up the bobcat could only respond, "Kiss my furry tail!"

Ms. Prickles, never took her eyes off Mayor, and saw that he was now tracking Billy Bob's steps.

She turned to the others and declared, "Okay, Rascals, I think it's time to go."

Before leaving, the animals agreed to reunite at Seward Pond, their regular hangout. It was time for a Rascals for the Environment meeting.

It was dusk when the Rascals arrived at the pond. Ms. Prickles arrived first, followed by Robin, Hoot, Patience, Roughhouse, and Chippy. Ronnie and Billy Bob were next. Now the crew was just waiting for Bandit. Billy Bob reported to everyone about the blueberries he had found in Mayor's garden. He suggested

MS. PRICKLES CALLS A RASCALS' MEETING

Bandit might be late because she had somehow found out about them. Their fears vanished as they saw the chubby raccoon come waddling onto the shore from the woods.

Ms. Prickles started the meeting.

"Let's start off with Billy Bob telling us all about what he discovered at Mayor's Cold River camp."

Billy Bob quickly relayed his finding the garden, the wigwams, the animal bones and hides, and the bow and arrows.

"This is truly amazing," Ms. Prickles said. "This man has been living right under our noses and we never knew about him. And from what Billy Bob describes of his camp, my guess is that Mayor is a hermit."

"A hermit crab?" Roughhouse blurted.

"Oh, no," Ms. Prickles gently corrected. "I think this man is a backwoodsman who lives alone for reasons only he could explain. This camp is his hermitage. His hideaway."

"He must be dangerous," Billy Bob said. "I mean, look at all the things he made out of dead animals."

"I know it does look bad, Billy Bob," said Ms. Prickles, "but, just like us, he needs to survive and animals help to give him the essentials he needs to live."

"Right, Ms. P.," Ronnie agreed. "We know that hunting, fishing and trapping are a part of life. Most of us are hunters in one way or another."

"Sure, you're both right," Patience said. "But how do we know if he is respectful of our environment or if he is a reckless woodsman, like the Freebooters?"

"You bring up a good point," Ms. Prickles said. "We'll do some detective work. You know, keep watch on him for the time being. We'll see how he treats our woods and the animals that live here."

"Good idea, Ms. P." Chippy said. "Why don't we begin right now and see what he does at night?"

They all agreed.

Sharing Soup with Mayor

When the Rascals returned to Mayor's camp they found the hermit leaning over a campfire, heating up some noodle soup in a pot.

Bandit volunteered to get a little closer to investigate. She insisted that her wanting to help had nothing to do with the delicious aroma wafting through the air.

While the hermit had his back turned, Bandit made her way over to the plank table near the stone fireplace. She hid underneath it. Her friends thought she was too close, but there was nothing they could do but watch and wait.

As Mayor finished warming up his supper, he carried the pot over to the table and sat down. Raising a spoonful of noodle soup to his mouth, he felt a sudden heavy nudge against his side pushing him off the bench. As he went down, the spoonful of soup flipped into the air, landing in his beard at the same time as the hermit hit the ground. Stunned, the noodle-soaked Mayor looked up to find a raccoon on his table boldly eating his soup right out of his pot!

BANDIT EATS BOLDLY RIGHT OUT OF THE POT

The hermit slowly reached for his soup pot, but then gracefully backed down, and retreated into his wigwam.

The other Rascals couldn't believe Bandit's boldness.

"I knew she was only after his food!" Ronnie cried.

"She'd better get back here and quick before Mayor grabs that bow and arrow and shoots her," Billy Bob said.

But Mayor just continued to watch from the doorway as Bandit finished off the last drop of soup, fumbled off the table, and waddled out of sight.

"Bandit," Ms. Prickles scolded as she returned to the others. "You took an awful risk and endangered yourself and us."

The raccoon apologized, but said she just didn't have any control over herself when it came to food.

"Let's end our investigation for the night," Ms. Prickles suggested.

The Rascals left the campsite, all, that is, except for Hoot. The owl decided to stay and keep watch over the hermit since he was normally up at that time anyway.

MAYOR AND HOOT SHARE A STORY

Hiding in Plain Sight

Perched on a tree limb near the Cold River camp, Hoot studied Mayor as the bearded man slowly rocked in his chair, peacefully reading a book by the firelight. The hermit soon began to get an eerie feeling that he was being watched. He glanced toward the outer edge of the camp and, not seeing anything, he slowly turned around in his seat, squinting out into the darkness behind him. He caught a glimpse of a shadow resting on a low-hanging limb. He looked closer and recognized the outline of an owl sitting ever so still, with its beaded eyes intently focused upon him.

Mayor put down his book, picked up a daily journal he had been keeping since he moved to the woods, and began to write in it. Because of his love of reading, Hoot was all the more interested. Forgetting all sensibilities, he lifted off, glided over toward Mayor, and landed on the back post of the rocker, giving him a clear view of the pages.

Mayor, surprised that the owl would be so daring, decided to act unconcerned and continued to write his entry.

Hoot pulled his glasses out from under his wing and began to read. He was quite fascinated. Mayor was writing about Bandit's earlier escapade. Then he was writing about an owl that was spying on Mayor. *Wow*, he thought. *I wonder who that could be?* Then he realized Mayor was writing about him. *Drat*! And he thought he was being so clever.

Bright and early the next day the Rascals met up with Hoot just outside the hermit's camp. He told them all about Mayor's journal. Bandit was quite flattered that she had made such an impression. Ms. Prickles thought it was interesting that Mayor kept his cool on realizing that there was an owl hovering over his shoulder. Most people would have been scared off.

While the others stayed to wait for Mayor to wake up, Hoot flew off to get some sleep. Roughhouse told Ms. Prickles that he had an idea he would like to try.

"If it's anything like Bandit's scheme with the soup…," Ms. Prickles warned.

"Oh, no, Ms. P.," Roughhouse assured her. "I had my fill of acorns this morning."

"What's the plan?" Chippy asked.

"Where is the one place a person would never expect to find a spy?" Roughhouse asked.

"Where?" his friends chimed.

"Right in plain sight!" the squirrel exclaimed.

Groans were heard all around.

Ms. Prickles, although somewhat wary of this plan, thought

Roughhouse deserved a chance to try out his idea.

Roughhouse scanned the area looking for the best spot to use and decided on the plank table. He scampered over, jumped up, and positioned himself on the edge of the tabletop. He looked over at the others, winked, and froze like Cold River on a winter day. If this plan was to work he couldn't afford to move one hair on his little body.

The rest of the Rascals thought he was crazy. Roughhouse was going to be discovered right away.

A few minutes passed before they heard the door to the hut open. Stepping out, Mayor gave a

ROUGHHOUSE HiDiNG iN PLAiN SiTE

loud morning yawn, stretched, and made a little bean toot. Next, the hermit walked over to the fireplace, bent down, picked up a stick, and stirred the still-warm embers of last night's fire. As the coals began to glow brightly, he placed some dry kindling over them, building the flame up strong enough to boil a kettle of water. All this occurred without Mayor ever noticing Roughhouse who was just five feet away standing perfectly still on the table.

The other animals began to think that maybe Roughhouse was on to something after all. But when Mayor poured a mug of coffee and stepped over to the table to drink it, they feared it was all over for their little buddy.

The Rascals all held their breath as the hermit lifted the steaming mug to his lips, stopped, and did a wide-eyed double-take in the direction of the squirrel.

Roughhouse, knowing that he had been discovered, but not wanting to look foolish in front of his friends, decided the best thing to do was to stay put and pretend that Mayor hadn't seen him.

Mayor, entertained by the stand the squirrel was making, decided to go about his business as if everything was normal. He sat undisturbed, sipping his coffee waiting to see what the little critter might do next. When the mug was empty, he slowly stood up, tipped his head toward Roughhouse as if saying, *so long*, then walked down the path to the river.

When Mayor was out of sight, Roughhouse skittered off the table and darted back to the others. They all patted him on the back and congratulated him on being so brave. Roughhouse was just relieved that his pals hadn't seemed to notice that Mayor had been on to him all along. This way he came out looking heroic. It also, secretly, gave the squirrel a new respect for this stranger who could have at any time, very easily, plucked him like a blade of grass.

"But Roughhouse," mocked Bandit, "what did you see that you couldn't have seen if you were in hiding with us?"

"The twinkle in the hermit's eye," the squirrel grinned.

Playing Drop and Retrieve

Later that afternoon Ms. Prickles sent Chippy back to Mayor's camp. She figured that if one Rascal watched at a time they might have a better chance of collecting more information.

Scampering into camp, Chippy, not seeing Mayor around, made his way down to the river's edge and found him sitting lazily on a log that had washed up on shore. On his lap was a bowl filled with nuts. The hermit was so intent on cracking open the nutshells with a stone hammer and eating the nutmeats that he didn't notice the chipmunk dodge underneath him into the hollow log.

Accidentally dropping a whole nut, Mayor reached down to retrieve it. Chippy couldn't believe his luck. Without thinking twice he dashed out, reaching the nut before Mayor had a chance to pick it up, clamped it between his teeth, and darted back into the log. Mayor chuckled after seeing this little episode. He then purposely dropped another nut to encourage the chipmunk to reappear.

They continued to play this game of "Drop and Retrieve"

CHIPPY SMILES THANKFULLY AT MAYOR

until Mayor was out of nuts and Chippy's cheeks were stuffed to the brim.

The chipmunk, now on the verge of toppling over, realized that the game was finished and poked his head out of the log. He briefly peered up at Mayor before running off to bury his nuts

Chippy was amazed at the stranger's generosity. There was no other explanation for Mayor dropping so many nuts, unless he was truly a clumsy man. Somehow the chipmunk doubted that. In fact, he was starting to believe that this hermit was quite a loveable and playful man.

Building a New Nest

The following morning Hoot flew to Seward Pond. He had just finished his second night of surveillance at Mayor's camp and wanted to report his observations to the others who were already gathered at the meeting ground.

Hoot reported that not much had gone on at the camp, although the hermit did write in his journal about Roughhouse and Chippy's mischievous acts.

"You know," said Ronnie, "I think Mayor is getting a real hoot out of all of us. No pun intended."

"Now, hold on. Don't be letting your hair down just yet," Ms. Prickles warned. "It is true that Mayor has been showing signs of decent behavior, but beware he is still a stranger."

"Ms. P. is right," Billy Bob declared. "You all remember the day I was tricked by a couple of hikers a few years back," stated the bobcat as he pointed to his raggedy ear. "That's the last time I come a-calling to the words '*kitty, kitty*'!"

The other Rascals tried to hide their giggles.

Ms. Prickles did not find it funny. "Billy Bob could have

been seriously hurt having let down his guard to those people. I had hoped his experience taught everyone a lesson."

The animals nodded their heads in solemn agreement.

The porcupine leader turned to the bird. "Now, Robin," she said, "would you be willing to build a temporary nest hidden within the camp? It might provide good backup for when one of us can't be there to observe."

Robin, thinking this was a grand idea, immediately flew off in search of a perfect spot to build her observation nest and by early afternoon half her nest was put together in the wigwam labeled Mrs. Rondeau's Kitchenette. She liked to be close to where there was the potential for bits of food.

When Robin was off gathering more material, Mayor happened to enter the wigwam and discovered the bird's work. He stood there awhile scratching his head, when suddenly he turned and headed toward the Beauty Parlor wigwam. Facing a mirror the hermit picked up a razor and gave himself a haircut. Then, after gathering up the silver-colored hair trimmings in a washbasin, he carried it over to the Kitchenette and gently placed it on a stump that was just in front of the wigwam. Looking satisfied with himself Mayor walked over by the fire, packed a bowl of tobacco, lit his pipe, and sat down to await whatever events might unfold.

It wasn't long before Robin came flying back carrying a few bits of twigs in her mouth. Gliding in for a smooth landing, she noticed a bowl near the wigwam that hadn't been there earlier. Cautiously, she fluttered up close to the stump, landed, and tentatively

MAYOR'S HAIR TRIMMINGS WILL MAKE A COZY NEST FOR ROBIN

reached out and felt the soft trimmings. Promptly she dropped the twigs in her beak. *What have we here*! she declared, quickly plucking up some of the silvery hair. Now her new nest would be warm and cozy.

Just then she noticed Mayor outside in his rocker watching her and smiling. She looked from the hermit to the trimmings twice before realizing what had happened. Mayor was sporting a new haircut.

Mayor chuckled as Robin gave him a flirtatious flick of her wings and a *"tweet"* before finishing her work. Soon she was settled into her new, snug nest. She knew she wasn't going to get any serious surveillance work done that day, all she wanted to do was cozy up and take a nice long nap. She didn't think that anyone who would give up their hair to a bird could be all that dangerous anyway.

She couldn't wait to tell Ms. Prickles about this.

11

Eye-to-Eye Over a Fish

Later that same day Mayor headed for a trout pond high on the shoulder of Mount Seward, never suspecting this was also the hangout for his recent animal visitors. Robin, all comfy in her new nest and slacking on her responsibilities, never noticed him leave. Because of this she was unable to warn Patience, who just happened to be alone at Seward Pond that afternoon.

The deer was frolicking about, playfully teasing the fish that were swimming around her hooves on the shallow grassy pond bottom. Mayor broke through the dense forest and wandered over to the water's edge. Both deer and man were oblivious to each other.

Looking all business-like, but seeming rather delighted about this new fishing ground, the hermit hooked a worm and cast his line out into the pond.

Patience's fun and games soon brought her close to Mayor. She was looking down, charging after one particular fish, while at the same time Mayor was excitedly reeling in his first catch of the day.

PATIENCE AND MAYOR COME
EYE TO EYE OVER A FISH

Patience came to an abrupt stop when suddenly she saw her fish rise up out of the water and dangle from the end of Mayor's fishing pole!

"Aaargh!" croaked the hermit as his eyes met the deer's. Both jumped back as if electrified.

A deer's first instinct is to run, so Patience took less than two slaps of a beaver's tail to dart out of the pond towards the woods. She paused long enough to give Mayor a quick look before dashing into the deep surrounding shelter of trees.

Mayor, who had also been startled, was totally flabbergasted by the unexpected meeting. He exhaled deeply as he watched the deer leave, and then turned back to his fishing.

Satisfied that she was safe and wasn't being followed, Patience bounded toward Cold River and Mayor's camp. When she reached the hermitage she headed directly toward the Kitchenette wigwam to interrogate Robin.

"Why didn't you warn me that Mayor was heading to our pond?" she sternly asked the sleepy-eyed bird.

"I didn't know he was," Robin replied. "But," she yawned, "I don't think we really need to worry about him. He seems quite friendly."

"He did seem just as surprised to see me as I was to see him," said Patience, starting to relax a little.

Patience left Robin to her nap and took the opportunity to promenade around the hermit's campground. She trotted through the open wigwams, meandered into the lush garden, and on her way out stopped to nibble on some pansies that were growing in an iron caldron close to Mayor's hut.

Anyone who takes the time to grow flowers can't be all that bad, she thought to herself.

BILLY BOB RUNNING FROM A FALLING CRATE

It's Raining... Supplies

The next morning Hoot returned from his nightly surveillance to report, yet again, what Mayor had written in his journal. This time Robin and Patience were the hot topic of the day. They both were quite pleased.

Hoot flew off to get his beauty sleep while the rest of the Rascals made their way back to the camp.

As they approached the site, they heard a rumbling noise off in the distance. Ronnie, who was leading the gang through the woods, came to a sudden stop, causing a domino effect. Each animal bumped into the one ahead of them. This proved to be most unfortunate for Bandit, because she was behind Ms. Prickles.

"Yow!" she squealed.

As the raccoon's friends were frantically pulling the quills out of her tummy, Roughhouse yelled, "Look!" There in the sky was a small plane circling above them. At the same time the hermit stepped out of his hut and watched as a few large crates were dropped from above.

Billy Bob noticed that the large boxes were headed straight toward them. "Run," he shouted.

The animals scattered. But before getting too far, three more boxes dropped. Luckily, no one was hit.

Mayor, waving up to the small plane, began to dance a jig around his cabin as the bush pilot made one last circle, dipped the plane's wings side to side in a *You are welcome* gesture, and flew off. He had been waiting for this airdrop for weeks. This was the only way of getting much-needed supplies without having to leave the woods. Gleeful, the aged hermit walked around gathering up the crates' contents. The wooden boxes had broken on contact with the ground spilling the items everywhere.

"What a funny man," Bandit commented as he watched Mayor dance about.

After seeing the plane leave, the Rascals reassembled. Peering over at Mayor, who was now standing among a cluster of canned and boxed goods, they watched as he retrieved the package's contents, sorted the food, refolded the clothing, and placed the items into different wigwams.

The Rascals were all quite fascinated.

"Boy," Ronnie commented. "If only we could have someone deliver supplies for us."

"We have all we need in the woods," Ms. Prickles said. "The hermit doesn't. Some things are just necessary for him to survive out here in the wild."

"It looks as though he uses all that he can from nature and

then has the rest sent," Billy Bob said. "He doesn't seem to waste a thing."

"That shows good character," Ms. Prickles said thoughtfully.

After his supplies were put away, Mayor made his way to his vegetable garden. He walked past the potato patch and entered the carrot rows. Gripping the green tops at ground level, he gently tugged a few long carrot roots from the soil. Wiping the soil from them on his pant leg, he arranged the bundle in a small pile on top of an overturned bucket placed between the rows, then turned, walked out of the garden and down the stringer of steps leading toward the river.

When Mayor left, Billy Bob and Ronnie offered to investigate the hermit's activities in his garden. As the volunteers crept into the garden their noses began to twitch and their eyes took on a crazed look. Exhilarated by the scent each dived toward two different spots in pure delight. "Yahoo! Yahoo!"

"IT'S CATNIP," Billy Bob loudly purred, as he pounced, then rolled onto the newly sowed plant.

Ronnie, over in the carrot pile, nibbled faster than a flicker of a hummingbird's wing, his mouth too full to say anything. Both were thrilled. Carrots and catnip were a luxury in the woods.

Suddenly, Mayor reappeared. The animals watched as the hermit stopped and witnessed the merry activity in the garden.

The hermit grinned in amusement. He looked happy that his newfound forest mates had found the small gifts so quickly.

43

BILLY BOB EATS TOO MUCH CATNIP

Careful not to scare the two happy critters away he traced a wide arc as he walked past the pair and over to his hut. They were so comical Mayor wanted to watch them enjoy themselves.

The Rascals, seeing this behavior from the stranger, looked at one another in astonishment. They couldn't believe he was allowing them to eat from his garden.

46

Freebooters Return

Billy Bob and Ronnie finished their treats and raced back to the others to tell them of their find. The entire band, except for Bandit, was overjoyed and a bit giddy to think that Mayor might be trying to befriend them.

"You don't really think that the hermit intended those as gifts for you two, do you?" the raccoon asked in a somewhat sarcastic tone.

"Yes, we do!" Billy Bob declared.

"You're just a sour old coon because he didn't leave any goodies out for you," Ronnie determined.

Crossing her arms, Bandit gave a loud, "Humph" as Ms. Prickles intervened announcing that there was to be a Rascals' meeting at Seward Pond immediately following dinner.

When the Rascals were gathered at the pond, Ms. Prickles asked that they all take turns giving their thoughts on Mayor. Robin was pleased by Mayor's kindness. Patience was impressed by his calmness. Hoot felt a bond with the hermit because of his books. Bandit was happy that he allowed her to eat his soup. Chippy, Billy Bob, and Ronnie thought he was a generous soul, and Roughhouse saw him as being "*cool*." When the gang finished their evaluation they realized that there was a unanimous belief that Mayor was a fair and decent man.

"I think," examined Ms. Prickles, "it will be a privilege to share our woods with this man."

"Yes," Chippy replied. "I hope we will also think of him as a friend."

"Ms. P.," Roughhouse asked. "How about we make Mayor an honorary member of our gang?"

"Well," Ms. Prickles hesitated, putting her thinking cap on. "He may be an honorable man but he really hasn't shown us any Rascal crusader traits."

"Aaah, shucks," exclaimed the squirrel, scraping his foot against the ground in disappointment and sending a cloud of dust straight up into Ronnie's face.

The rabbit, breaking into a coughing fit, didn't hear the rustling sounds that came from the woods near the pond, but the others grew quiet to listen. They were thinking that maybe it was Mayor coming back for more trout until deep voices were heard followed by gunshots. The Rascals quickly hid. Each held their breath, silently waiting, while carefully scanning the woods to see what was coming.

Moments later, five gruff-looking men entered the clearing wearing soiled clothes and camouflage hunting caps. Each had on a knapsack and was carrying a rifle!

THE FREEBOOTERS ARE BACK

The Rascals were alarmed. Their worst fears had come true. "The Freebooters are back!" they gasped.

These men did not treat the natural environment fairly. They shot at anything that moved, camped in the woods leaving litter on the ground, and left fires burning — never bothering to extinguish them.

It was common knowledge that a number of wildfires had started from the Freebooters' unkempt campfires. These men cared little for the beauty of the forest and its inhabitants. All animals feared them. The Rascal gang knew they were in grave danger.

The gang watched as the Freebooters set up camp near the shore of their beautiful high mountain pond. They dropped their backpacks, unpacked their gear, put up tents, laid out sleeping bags, and then went off in search of firewood. As the shadows of the trees marched in line with the setting sun the animals came together discuss what should be done.

"We all know how much of a threat these men are to our forest," Ms. Prickles stated. "We need to run these Freebooters out of our home once and for all."

Rallied by their resolve that these men were not like normal hikers, anglers, hunters, loggers, and tourists, the Rascals for the Environment gang's instincts kicked in. Their fears took a backseat to their determination. There and then the gang resolved to chase the Freebooters out of the Adirondack Mountains. *Forever.*

Rascals' Revenge

While the Freebooters were collecting firewood, the Rascals brainstormed ways to get rid of the ruffians. Within a short time they had devised a clever operation.

"Okay, everyone," Ms. Prickles commanded. "We all have a job to do. So, on the count of three lets begin. One… two…three!"

Ms. Prickles ran to the water's edge and scooped up two tin cans of water, and carefully made her way over to Patience, who had just propped up one of the Freebooter's guns so her porcupine accomplice could dump water into the barrel. The two of them continued this exercise until all the rifle barrels were filled with water.

Robin flew to the large open kettle full of water that the men had set by the newly made fire pit to use for coffee and soup. With full knowledge of her action, Robin, jumping from the rim into the liquid, proceeded to cleanse herself as she often did in a puddle of rainwater. Satisfied she had thoroughly washed, she rolled over on her back and kicked around her

ROBIN BATHING IN THE FREEBOOTERS' SUPPER

new-found "swimming pool," making sure plenty of her feathers were left behind before exiting the pot.

Chippy went off into the woods in search of burrs. His plan was to place the sharp, clingy seedpods inside each of the men's sleeping bags. As he came back to the shore, he quickly dodged back and forth between the pile of burrs he had made and the Freebooters' tents. But, as he was finishing the delivery of his "presents" to the last tent, the men returned.

Ms. Prickles, Patience, and Robin had enough time to dash back into the trees without being seen, but poor Chippy was trapped in the nylon tent. There was no way to escape unnoticed. The Rascals had no choice but to leave him behind until they could figure out a way to free him. They just hoped he would not be discovered.

The forest became wrapped in a dark cloak as evening arrived. *It's time for some action, Freebooters,* the Rascals thought before setting out into the darkness. *The night is ours.* As they watched the moon rise and heard the call of a distant night bird the gang, one by one, tiptoed from the surrounding trees to the edge of the Freebooters' camp. The vandals were lounging around a campfire. The water pot where Robin had performed her bath was propped up on top of a gridiron over the flames of the fire. While the men were laughing and telling bad jokes they haphazardly scooped stew from the pot into wide metal bowls. The Rascals watched as each Freebooter spooned the food into his mouth. Almost in unison, the men began spitting out the contents. Pieces of carrots, peas, and meat sprayed in all directions.

Sputtering, one man shouted, "What in the firing blue blazes is this awful taste?"

"I don't think it was the stew," said another, as he tried to clean himself up.

"Look here!" shouted another as he tipped the cooking pot and shined a flashlight on the steaming contents.

"Why, there's bird feathers in this stew pot!" a very angry Freebooter yelled.

"If that there bird comes back again," the same man warned, "I'm going to blow that feathery creature right out of the sky!"

"Aw, lets just call it a night, fellers," another suggested, feeling deprived of his supper and now not interested in his nightly cup of coffee. "The evening's been ruined."

The men made their way to their tents. The Rascals watched anxiously as a Freebooter entered the tent that held Chippy. *Would he notice their little chipmunk friend?* All was quiet for the first few minutes, until a roar broke the silent night. One by one the men began running out of their tents tossing out their sleeping bags, screaming and yelling, dancing and hopping as they held onto their tender backsides. *"Hooray for Chippy,"* the Rascals chimed as the Freebooters plucked at their pajama-clad bottoms trying to pull off the needle-like burrs. As the men leaped about Chippy scampered out of his prison-like setting, and clapped his front paws. Then he kicked a foot full of dirt into the stew pot, readjusted his ball cap, and scurried over to the others.

"Goll darn! Bloomin' britches!" an angry red-faced Freebooter screamed. "How, in the name of my flea-bitten dog, could burrs get into our sleeping bags?"

"Did y'all see any other people in the woods?" another asked while yanking some prickly burrs from his socks.

"Naw, ain't seen anyone, but we're not gonna put up with these tricks. Come tomorrow we're gonna find who's doin' this."

CHiPPY HAS A PLAN

With their burr-filled sleeping bags now in a pile, they returned to their tents, settling in for a less than comfortable night.

An hour passed before Roughhouse felt safe enough to sneak over to one of the tents and gnaw at the nylon, making a hole big enough for a prowler to enter. He was waiting for Ronnie to find a skunk to carry out their plan.

Leaving the snoring Freebooters behind, Roughhouse tiptoed back to the shrubs and gave Bandit an all-clear sign to enter the camp. Bandit boldly marched into the Freebooters' camp. She thought that if she stole the men's food supply, it would force them to pack up and leave the woods. Ms. Prickles agreed to this plan only if Bandit promised to share the goods with the other forest animals.

Bandit made a beeline straight for the backpacks. Skillfully she unzipped each pack, pulled out the food bag, and stuffed the best morsels into her mouth before dragging the rest over to the gang.

"Nice job, Bandit," Ms. Prickles complimented. "Everyone take some."

Soon Ronnie returned accompanied by a skunk, who shared the Rascals wish to rid the woods of the Freebooters. Roughhouse pointed toward the hole he had chewed in the tent. The skunk, brimming with anticipation, and knowing just what to do, trotted over and entered. Quick as a wink the skunk unloaded her powerful fragrance, dashed outside, nodded to the Rascals, *the deed's been done*, and disappeared into the woods.

Instantly they heard loud coughing. Frantic movement soon followed as the man tried to unzip the tent. He finally tumbled out, gasping for air. The noise awakened the other men, who scrambled out of their tents to see what had happened. The question was solved quickly, since the skunk odor was spreading like dandelions in a wide-open field.

Fear of Night Noises

The Rascals decided to stay through the night. The spectacle was comical but the situation was not. Surely there was more work to be done before they were to be rid of these villains. The Freebooters ended up sleeping in the fresh open air hoping that would ease the smell. It didn't.

In the dark of the night as the Freebooters lay on the cold, hard ground, Hoot flew to an overhanging tree branch above the restless men and began to make loud, creepy sounds.

"Whooooeessse, Whoooessse," he hooted. "Wheeezzooo, Wheeezzooo."

"What 'sat?" a bewildered Freebooter sat up and questioned.

"Sounds like an owl with a head cold," one man joked as the others laughed. Hoot was not pleased.

Robin whispered, "Come on, gang, we can help Hoot out with this."

Soon, a chorus of strange and frightening sounds was heard around Seward Pond.

"Eeerrowl. Zeeeak. Noorrk. Noorrk. Brrowl."

FREEBOOTERS HUDDLE
IN FEAR OF NIGHT NOISES

The tough and rowdy Freebooters were shaken and scared. They sat up, made a grab for their guns and aimed into the shadowy forest. But instead of hearing a loud popping sound from their rifles, the guns made a weak, *blip*, *blip* noise. The water Ms. Prickles had poured into the barrels had soaked the ammunition and caused the guns to misfire. When the men pulled the triggers all that happened were dull explosions followed by spurts of water trickling out of the ends.

The men stood with their rifles in open-mouthed amazement until one of them hollered, "These good-fer-nothin' woods are haunted!"

Skunk smell or no skunk smell, the outwitted men dove into the nearest tent, huddling together against the menacing sounds until the first light of dawn. Not a wink of sleep was had by any of them.

Mayor to the Rescue

Waking up in the early dawn hours the weary Freebooters left their tent. Backs to each other and eyes darting out toward the still dark woods, they slowly made their way down to the river to bathe. The men undressed, jumped into the chilly pond water, and began scrubbing themselves raw. The skunk smell from the previous night was still quite potent. They used mud as soap and floating bark as washcloths. As they all dove underwater for one final rinse, one man surfaced wearing a lily pad atop his head. He looked about in confusion, then suddenly turned toward shore. "Hey, guys, look at that rabbit and bob-cat." He pointed. "They're taking off with our duds!"

While the men had been washing up, Billy Bob and Ronnie had made a quick decision to snatch up the Freebooters' clothing and take off with it.

Naked, the men clamored out of the pond, picking up rocks, sticks, and anything else they could lay their hands on and began throwing them at Ronnie and Billy Bob. As the two tried to dodge the flying objects, the rest of the Rascals gang came out of hiding and ran wildly about hoping to confuse and distract the Freebooters.

This chaotic scene was taking place just at the moment Mayor stepped into the clearing. Thinking he was in for a peaceful morning of trout fishing, the hermit was shocked at the baffling sight that he encountered. Wild, angry men running around buck naked were chasing after his new woodland neighbors. Quickly he pulled out his bow and arrows. "Halt, you green-timber sneakens!" he yelled, pointing them at the men.

Both the Rascals and the Freebooters turned toward the old hermit. Relief flowed across the Rascals' faces.

Seeing the old woodsman with his long white beard and his baggy trousers made the ruffians laugh out loud. They weren't fearful of him. They were bigger and tougher and younger.

"What are you doing in my neck of the woods?" Mayor demanded in his most unpleasant voice.

"Bugger off, old timer," they cussed back, showing no fear toward Mayor.

"Yo ho, I warn you, I may be old in years but I can outwear all of you."

His strong sounding voice had in it the fury of a winter storm. Taking into account what happened to them the night before, and now this, they started to weaken. They dropped their rocks and sticks and raised their hands up in surrender.

Mayor delivered his final warning. " NEVER return to our forest again!"

The men cast a puzzling glance toward the animals and the hermit standing united and scrambled to fetch their packs. Cold and shivering they hurried out of the woods. On bare feet they stumbled through trees and brambles not stopping till they reached the safety of their vehicles.

Once the Freebooters were out of sight, the woodland gang let out a collective sigh. Peace filled their minds as elation sunk in. *The Freebooters were gone forever*. Mayor and the animals felt a sudden bond having each played a part in ridding their homeland of scoundrels.

Mayor made the first move. Walking around until he found a good stick, he began digging a hole. Using their paws, claws, and hooves to scrap away the dirt the Rascals joined in. When the hole was deep enough, Mayor dropped all of the Freebooters' guns in and then refilled the hole, packing down the earth. The hermit tossed down his stick, wiped the dirt from his hands, gave a wave to the animals, and headed back to camp.

Ms. Prickles, facing her crew, voiced her liking. "Now I believe Mayor deserves to be an honorary member of our gang, for today he has shown us some real good Rascal crusader traits!"

"Hooray for Mayor," everyone shouted. "Hip, hip hooray!"

PAN-E-CAKES

The Newest Member of the Rascals

It is a rare occurrence when one receives honorary membership in the Rascals for the Environment gang. So, when the event does occur it is not taken lightly. The Rascals each spend much time thinking up a gift to offer to the honoree during the ceremony. They each decide on a memento that best describes a part of them.

After spending much of the day carefully making their selections, the animals, carrying their gifts, made their way along the now worn path to Mayor's camp.

As they drew closer, they were met with the most mouth-watering smell they had ever encountered. Not a word was spoken as the animals abruptly dropped their precious mementos and hastily followed their noses.

The heavenly aroma led the gang straight to Mayor's wigwam and found him leaning over a hot stove, flipping something on a skillet. Their eyes wandered to a plate of food on top of the plank table.

"Pan-e-cakes!" screeched Bandit as she flew over to the huge stack, the others right behind her.

Mayor turned to find his table filled with lovable woodland critters. He had purposefully made enough pancakes to share. Piling a few more on the plate, he made his way over to his new friends. He squeezed in between Ronnie and Billy Bob and they all settled down to enjoy their very own "Adirondack Feast."

Evening fast approached and found the Rascals, with bellies full, dozing around the campfire. Mayor was nearby rocking in his chair playing a few tunes on his fiddle. He, too, soon nodded off.

Ms. Prickles was first to awaken. She quietly nudged everyone else and collected the gifts to bring over to their beloved hermit.

As they circled around him, Mayor of Cold River slowly opened his eyes. Ms. Prickles, walking up to the woodsman laid down one of her quills at his feet. Bandit followed with a handful of blueberries. Billy Bob was next with a fur ball. Robin and Hoot came offering each a feather. Ronnie gave him a tuft of tail hair. Patience offered flowers to replace the ones she had eaten earlier from his caldron. And Roughhouse and Chippy brought Mayor some of their favorite nuts from their stash.

When the Rascals were finished the hermit nodded in understanding. He looked around at his friends then up toward the tall moonlit tips of the Adirondack Mountains. Never in his whole life had he felt so blessed.

As for the Rascals, they were delighted to be able to call this man their friend. This opened up a whole new world of hope and inspiration for their future battles to protect the environment.

This was nature at its best.

BANDIT'S GIFT OF BLUEBERRIES

67

The character, Mayor, in
The Rascals for the Environment,
is loosely based on Noah John Rondeau,
a well-known Adirondack hermit who did,
in fact, live in the woods in several
roughly constructed "wigwams."
He did have a "special" relationship with nature,
but also did like people—on his terms.